WHEN THE RIGHT ONE

#WTROC

Greg M. Davis Sr.

Dedication

This book and collections of **#wtroc** is dedicated to those who, like myself, still believe in love!

I also wrote this for those who might have felt like giving up on love, because you have been hurt in the process and made some bad choices.

I want to dedicate this to my favorite girl my baby girl, Micah Kimberly Davis. I am praying and believing she will find *The Right One*!

Introduction

Success is not success, until you have failed at something. Most people who speak from authority, on a given subject, speak from failures, in their lives. Experts are experts, because they have first-hand research or knowledge on a specific subject. This is not by theory, but from true experience.

About 3 years ago my brother and sister, Keith and Carla, had just started an internet radio show at one of our restaurants downtown. I wanted to go support them and rode my bike downtown to the show. Anyone who knows or follows me knows that I love working out with a good bike ride. On this particular day, I was feeling down about my current relationship status of being single. I had absolutely no prospects. I was so tired of meeting people who only wanted to play games. Can you relate? Seemingly, those who wanted a relationship I found I had no interest for one reason or another.

I began to think about my failed marriage and failed relationships and began to take responsibility for my part of the issues that arose. I wanted to be in a relationship, but didn't have in mind what I wanted in a woman. I began think of what I didn't want, because I had quite enough experience with that.

4

I was so weary of failure. Whether on my part or their part, it was still failure. I definitely not playing the blame game, because it's always both parties fault. There were a couple dynamics I was experiencing. Someone either gave up or didn't want the relationship or because of being separate and lonely one probably shouldn't have been with the person, in the first place.

When I got to the live radio show, Keith and Carla were talking about relationships that day. As we had often done on my show. I sat in a corner waiting for them to start and began to post on social media. Daily, I would post encouragement with the hashtag #gogetit, but today I decided I would send a tweet about relationships. I don't even remember what the first post stated, but the theme was **When The Right One Comes**.

I went on for an hour posting when the right one comes this and when the right one comes that. All of sudden, my timelines were going crazy on all social media platforms, with people's opinions of liking the post and retweets. I posted all evening of when the right one comes. My followers were blowing up my timeline with responses and thanking me. They were telling me I was on fire. To my own surprise, I didn't know where all this was coming from. I didn't realize I had so much in me, regarding the subject of relationship.

5

Then I realized, I was tweeting my own failures and m desires regarding the right one. I was not really looking for the right one, but sharing who I felt wasn't and what I felt the right one looked like.

Of course, not everyone was happy about my posts and opinions. There were those who felt, because I had been in a relationship with them that I was talking about them or throwing off on them personally. This was not the case! I was merely sharing my personal feelings and what I felt about the right one.

When The Right One Comes is collection of my experiences, failures and desires. It is also me thinking out loud and sharing it with others on my social media platform. The reason I think it's so popular is because people can relate and immediately identify. If everyone would be honest, we all have the desire to have the right one. The truth is so many, like me, have made bad choices in the areas of dating and marriage. Anyone could write these quotes, because all of us have been in relationships that we have regretted or are even regretting.

I don't claim to be an expert on relationships, but I have failed enough in the area to know more than I did 20 years ago. I may not know what the right one completely looks like yet, but I do know what the right one doesn't look like.

6

I have been told by many these quote have saved them from making bad choices and decisions, in their search of the right one. I believe everyone deserves to be happy, with the right one.

One thing I am for sure is that it takes much longer for the right one to come then settling for the wrong one, but it's worth the wait.

I'm sure you would agree, if you just would have waited and didn't ignore the warning signs and red flags. If you would've paid attention when you saw them, you would have cried less tears.

There are so many who are hiding behind statements like "I'm doing me". "I'm successful without someone". "I'm getting me together." For the most part, these are fear statements. Fear of it is not going to work. I'm not going to be hurt again. But, you won't know unless you take a go at it. May be this is the right one or may be it is not, but you will never know, unless you try. If nothing else, it will help you to know what you don't want.

7

As you read this book and these quotes, stay hopefully optimistic. Don't just read my quotes, but be inspired to write your own, from your own experiences and failures. Most of all write what you expect and believe what you write and what you want them to be and they will manifest in your life.

Enjoy my collection of thoughts of #WTROC.

The Collection

No. 1

Don't be so desperate for the right one that you settle for the wrong one! #WTROC

No. 2

When the right one comes, you will not only love them, but you will _like_ them! #WTROC

No. 3

Find yourself, before you find the right one! #WTROC

No. 4

Increase who you are and it will increase who the right one will be!
#WTROC

No. 5

Ladies, when the right man comes, you won't have to ask for anything, because he will give you everything! #WTROC

No. 6

When the right one comes, they won't be just a lot of talk, but they will be full of action and substance! #WTROC

No. 7

You have not enjoyed relationships, in the past, because they weren't the right ones. #WTROC

No. 8

When the right one comes you will know that you didn't just settle, but that you got what you wanted and needed! #WTROC

No. 9

Don't make the right one pay the bill of the hurt you suffered, with the wrong one! #WTROC

No. 10

Take less time thinking about the right one and more time preparing for the right one! #WTROC

No. 11

If you're busy and they're not, they may not be the right one. They have too much time to worry about what you're doing! #WTROC

No. 12

Only time will bring the right one, not anything else! #WTROC

No. 13

When the right one comes it doesn't mean there won't be challenges, but it does mean you can work anything out together! #WTROC

No. 14

When right one comes you will talk about it and not argue about it! #WTROC

No. 15

Maybe the real reason the right man hasn't come is because, you're not ready! #WTROC

No. 16

Stop trying to rush to get married, without being friends first! #WTROC

No. 17

Ladies when the right one comes, you won't have to change him or fix him up! #WTROC

No. 18

Take time to be healed, so when the right one comes you won't have a sick relationship. #WTROC

No. 19

If you're not right, the right one can come and they still will not be the right one because you're not right or ready. #WTROC

No. 20

Maybe you have come across the right one, but you were not ready which turned him into the wrong one? #WTROC

No. 21

You can't be wrong trying to find the right one!
#WTROC

No. 22

When the right one comes, they won't get on your
last nerve! #WTROC

No. 23

When the right one comes, they will be incapable of
leaving you alone! #WTROC

No. 24

When the right one comes, the two of you will be in
sync in every area of your life and not out of sync!
#WTROC

No. 25

When the right one comes, you won't have to put
your vision on hold. They will support it! #WTROC

No. 26

Don't be bitter, because of all of the wrong ones. Be better, so you will be healed, when the right one comes! #WTROC

No. 27

Be better, because of all the wrong ones; not bitter, so you will be well and healed when the right one comes! #WTROC

No. 28

You decide to do the right thing and the right one will come! #WTROC

No. 29

When the right one comes even though they are the right one, it still requires hard work! #WTROC

No. 30

When the right one comes, intimacy between the two of you will be just as important as everything else. #WTROC

No. 31

When the right one comes, they won't be a project, fix me up or a rescue. They will come ready, willing and able! BAM! #WTROC

No. 32

When the right one comes, he's not there to tear down walls of your past relationships, but to build up a new one with you. #WTROC

No. 33

This year, if you would just live in the moment of being single and not worry about when the right one is coming, they would be here before you know it. #WTROC

No. 34

Until you find someone to love you how about you love you, so when the right one comes you know how it feels to really be loved! #WTROC

No. 35

When the right one comes, it will be worth starting over again! No hesitation. No reservations! #WTROC

No. 36

This year you will know when the right one comes, because they will be ready to shut down all games and you will be the only one! #WTROC

No. 37

Love you. Make you happy. Take you out. Enjoy your life. Learn you. Find yourself. Be excited about you. So, when the right one comes, you got all this covered. #WTROC

No. 38

Today I start working on me & becoming the right one so when the right one comes I will be ready! #WTROC

No. 39

This will be a year of getting me together. So, when the right one comes, they will have a complete person. #WTROC

No. 40

This year, I will be made whole. So, when the right one comes, they won't get a broken and bitter person. #WTROC

No. 41

Before next year comes, I will let go of meaningless relationships that I know will never go anywhere #WTROC

No. 42

Lord heal my heart. So, when the right one comes, I will be the best me that I can be. #WTROC

No. 43

This year, I will not lose me, in order to gain you. #WTROC

No. 44

This year, I will not settle for you, because of loneliness and being desperate for attention! #WTROC

No. 45

This year, if I can't be treated like I was designed to be treated, then I will treat me until they come. #WTROC

No. 46

This year, I will not miss out on the right one, because of what you did to me last year. #WTROC

No. 47

This year, I will not look for you to complete or fulfill me, but to compliment who I am already. #WTROC

No. 48

Today, I end the cycle of being in relationship that offer nothing and close the door to hurt and abandonment. #WTROC

No. 49

Today, I am opening the door to new possibilities. I am in expectation that this is the year that the right one will come. #WTROC

No. 50 Part 1

There is nothing to brag about when you are successful doing well and got it going on, but you are all alone and have no one to share it with!
#WTROC

Part 2

Real success is when you got it all together and someone to share it and you are willing to admit it.
#WTROC

Part 3

Life without anyone to share it with is not living life to its fullest potential.

No. 51

Stop trying to make things happen with someone who's not interested in your NEXT! #WTROC

No. 52

When you know your worth, you won't settle for worthless relationships! #WTROC

No. 53

I'm not going to be your fall back, when I can be your main all the time! *#WTROC*

No. 54

Maybe the right one is right under your nose, but you don't notice them, because you're looking in other places! *#WTROC*

No. 55

Can't find them, until I find myself! *#WTROC*

No. 56

You can't embrace a new relationship in your life because you allow the old ones to continue to haunt you! *#WTROC*

No. 57

Ladies, don't scare the right man off with the defense mechanism of your mouth! *#WTROC*

No. 58

When you're single, there's no rush or pressure to jump into the wrong thing. That's the beauty of it you can explore your options! *#WTROC*

No. 59

You can't stay with the wrong one, in hopes the right one will rescue you! Leave! #WTROC

No. 60

Don't punish the right one for what the wrong one did! They don't deserve it! #WTROC

No. 61

To be the right one to your man, you have to be all things to him, so he won't look elsewhere for what he's not getting! #WTROC

No. 62

If it doesn't feel right, go with your first feeling. It is never wrong! They are not the right one! No time to waste. #WTROC

No. 63

Ladies, God is sending the right one in your life with money and resources to help carry the load and the burden that you have been under for so long! #WTROC

No. 64

Don't have your priorities backwards. Finding you first then the right one is the right order, not the other way around! #WTROC

No. 65

When you have the right one, they will never leave you no matter what they will stick and stay! #WTROC

No. 66

This year I will enjoy my space, until it is filled with the right one! I won't settle for putting the wrong one in my space! #WTROC

No. 67

This year, focus on friendship, because the right one will want to be your best friend above anything else. That's where it all starts. #WTROC

No. 68

This year, I will know the right one, because they value my time, who I am and what I do and won't complain about any of it! #WTROC

No. 69

When you are not in a relationship, it's not time to focus on why you're not, but it's time to focus more on improving you. #WTROC

No. 70

This year, I am over the hurt and bitterness of relationships of the past that didn't work and believing I will not leave this year without the right one! #WTROC

No. 71

When it gets hard to love someone close up and personal, then you have to love them from far away and in personal! #WTROC

No. 72

Chose to be by yourself and happy, rather than with someone and miserable! #WTROC

No. 73

Why do you keep trying to go back? There's a reason why they are your Ex! #WTROC

No. 74

Men think they can rescue women and women think they can change men! Neither can do either!
#WTROC

No. 75

Ladies, they are who they're going to be. So, why do you keep trying to make them someone else!
#WTROC

No. 76

You want to stop a man from his games be the right one! If not, he will keep playing! #WTROC

No. 77

Become friends and confidants and it will last!
#WTROC

No. 78

We keep going in the same viscous cycles, because we're trying to make someone the right one that's not! #WTROC

No. 79

If everyone you meet, you take out on them what the last one did to you, you will never find the right one. #WTROC

No. 80

If it's too easy to get chances are it's too good to be true! #WTROC

No. 81

Ladies, they treat you like you allow them to treat you! #WTROC

No. 82

When they are the right one, their texts, emails, calls and visits will be a joy to receive, not a headache! #WTROC

No. 83

Stop trying to force someone into your life, when they are the right one there's not a force! #WTROC

No. 84

Stop trying to make him the right one either he is or he's not! #WTROC

27

No. 85

If they are getting on your nerves in the dating process, it will not get better! They are not the one! #WTROC

No. 86

If it doesn't work, don't make it work! #WTROC

No. 87

Finding the right one doesn't mean someone perfect, but it does mean they are best them they can be! #WTROC

No. 88

Stop trying to make things happen with someone who's not interested in your NEXT! #WTROC

No. 89

Decide whether you want a project or you want them already together! Some people don't have time for projects, at this point in life! #WTROC

No. 90

Refuse to make the same relationship mistakes you already made, by not falling for the same craziness! #WTROC

No. 91

Never be sad on days like this, because you are by yourself. Rather, be by yourself today than to be with the wrong one! #WTROC

No. 92

When you know your value and worth, you don't have to run after anything or anybody it will come to you! #WTROC

No. 93

Stop chasing them, if they won't slow down to be caught! #WTROC

No. 94

If they have not put in the time before Valentine's Day, then they are not the right one and are undeserving of your time! #WTROC

No. 95

How many red flags do you need waved in your face, before you know they aren't the right one! #WTROC

No. 96

A sign that the right one has arrived is they will bring peace into your life and not stress! #WTROC

No. 97

Ladies, when the right man comes you won't have to worry about where he is at night or any other time! #WTROC

No. 98

When you're in Love with just being in love, it's not enough. You will never find the right one! #WTROC

No. 99

You knew when he opened his mouth and what came out of it that he wasn't the right one. Red Flag! Not the one! #WTROC

No. 100

Ladies, stop being bitter about what all the wrong men did. Thank them for showing you what you don't deserve and want! #WTROC

No. 101

Decide to stop looking for the right one and they will show up, when you don't even expect them to! Get ready! #WTROC

No. 102

Pursuing is not running after somebody. The other person has to be a willing and able participant! #WTROC

No. 103

Making you smile. Making you happy. Making you laugh. Making you blush. Making you giggle. Making you feel warm inside. All are signs of the right one! #WTROC

No. 104

If what they are being is no better then what you have had, that's a red flag and they are not the right one. Not even a consideration! #WTROC

No. 105

If everyone is guarded and has walls up, then how will you ever get the right one? #WTROC

No. 106

Cleaning cob webs of the hurt, pain, bad feelings, anger and the feeling of betrayal that has been in my heart is necessary, when you are getting ready to move forward to the right one! #WTROC

No. 107

Find someone to enjoy life with. Someone to laugh with. Share with. Be yourself with. They will love you just the way you are. Now that's the right one! #WTROC

No. 108

Were they really the right one or were they the choice of your loneliness? The right one would still be there! #WTROC

No. 109

Just because they want you doesn't mean you have to want them back! Waiting on the right one you will have to learn how to say... No Thanks! #WTROC

No. 110

A sign that the right one has come is that we are going in the same direction! We are in sync. We are dreaming together! #WTROC

No. 111

If they're the right one, you won't have to work hard to be with them. It will fall into place naturally. #WTROC

No. 112

When the right one comes, you are never too busy to talk, text or spend time with them because they take priority! #WTROC

No. 113

If you're waiting for the perfect person and for the perfect relationship, you may have a long wait. Neither exists! #WTROC

No. 114

Don't give up who you are to for somebody else who don't know who they are! #WTROC

No. 115

At some point, you have to just say they are NOT the right one!!!! #WTROC

No. 116

If you weren't lonely would they still be the one? That's the deciding factor! #WTROC

No. 117

Ask yourself. Is this person worth the time and investment to move forward with a relationship? #WTROC

No. 118

Just because you're ready for the right one doesn't mean everyone else is! #WTROC

No. 119

If they are the right one, you don't have to persuade or make them be with you! #WTROC

No. 120

When the right one comes, they will not only be an emotion and physical support, but they will be a financial support to the relationship! #WTROC

No. 121

The right one will go out of their way for you, without asking any procrastination or hesitation! #WTROC

No. 122

If they don't identify you as the right one in their life, they are not the right one for you! It has to be mutual. #WTROC

No. 123

When the right one comes, she won't have a sharp tongue and he won't be disrespectful! #WTROC

No. 124

A true sign that they are the right one is when you go to get rid of them and they are always on your mind and they never give up! #WTROC

No. 125

When the right one comes, they are adaptable and pliable. #WTROC

No. 126

When the right one comes, they won't treat you like the last one! #WTROC

No. 127

Believe it or not a signal they are the right one is there will be outside adversity on every hand! Don't run. Press in! #WTROC

No. 128

You can talk until you're blue in the face, but the heart wants what it wants!

No. 129

The right one will never take away or tear down, but build up and add to whatever you are doing already! #WTROC

No. 130

When you are each other's right one, you don't have to compromise or change anything. You will be just right for each other! #WTROC

No. 131

The right one can call you and see you at all times. Because you're the only one. #WTROC

No. 132

If you don't know what you want then you won't recognize, when the right one comes! #WTROC

No. 133

When the right one comes, they will be committed to the relationship! #WTROC

No. 134

When the right one comes you won't have to fight through layers of their past! #WTROC

No. 135

When the right man comes, your days of wondering, if he's faithful, is over! He will be a faithful man! #WTROC

No. 136

When the right man comes, you can dry your eyes. Your crying over someone will be over! #WTROC

No. 137

When the right one comes, there will be nothing you will be afraid to discuss with them! #WTROC

No. 138

When the right one comes, there will be nothing you won't forgive one another for! #WTROC

No. 139

When the right one comes, your lives are an open book to each other! #WTROC

No. 140

When the Right one comes, there's nothing that you won't share from them about your past present or future! #WTROC

No. 141

When the right one comes, there will be shared goals in each other's future! #WTROC

No. 142

When the right one comes there will be a mutual interest for one another! #WTROC

No. 143

When the right one comes you will ask not what they can do for you but what you can do for them! #WTROC

No. 144

When the right one comes you will vibe with them! #WTROC

No. 145

When the right one comes there will be incredible chemistry between the both of you! #WTROC

No. 146

When the right one comes, giving up on each other will not be an option! #WTROC

No. 147

When the right one comes, you won't have to teach them or tell them how to please you! #WTROC

No. 148

When the right one comes, it won't be a one- sided relationship. It will be beneficial to both parties! #WTROC

No. 149

When the right one comes, you won't have to figure out what you're doing for the weekend! #WTROC

No. 150

When the right one comes, it won't be a dysfunctional relationship! Total functionally! #WTROC

No. 151

When the right one comes, weekends won't be long enough to spend with each other! #WTROC

No. 152

When the right one comes, they won't treat you like a child, but a partner! #WTROC

No. 153

When the right man comes, he will have a heart not just for you, but your children! #WTROC

No. 154

When the right lady comes, she won't just be in it for what she can get, but willing to give her all! #WTROC

No. 155

When the right man comes, he would have put away childish ways! #WTROC

No. 156

When the right man comes, he won't have a problem taking responsibility! #WTROC

No. 157

When the right man comes, he will be a good listener! Always listening how he can enhance your life! #WTROC

No. 158

Real love knows how to say, it's my fault and I'm sorry! #WTROC

No. 159

When the right man comes, he won't have a problem with saying he's sorry, when he's wrong! #WTROC

No. 160

When the right lady comes, she won't be stubborn! #WTROC

No. 161

When the right man comes, he won't have a problem taking responsibility! #WTROC

No. 162

When the right man comes, he will be a real man!
#WTROC

No. 163

When the right one comes, there will be a mutual
respect and admiration for each other's careers!
#WTROC

No. 164

When the right one comes, there will be such a bond
you will be able to sense and feel each other.
#WTROC

No. 165

When the right one comes, there will be true
partnership working together, not separate.
#WTROC

No. 166

When right one comes, there will be true friendship
first! #WTROC

No. 167

When the right one comes, anything can be fixed between the two of you #WTROC

No. 168

When the right man comes, you will be able to trust him with your feelings and emotions. He won't take advantage of them! #WTROC

No. 169

When the right one comes, they won't be a burden, but a blessing to your life! #WTROC

No. 170

When the right one comes, you will be amazed to what real love can be like! #WTROC

No. 171

When the right one comes, all bad memories fade away! #WTROC

No. 172

When the right one comes, no more broken heart! #WTROC

No. 173

Bro don't be upset, when a woman is beating you at your own game. After all, we taught them through all they have gone through. #WTROC

No. 174

Maybe you can't get the right one, because you haven't healed yet from the wrong one?!?! #WTROC

No. 175

Don't end up with the wrong one, because you can't recognize when the right one comes! #WTROC

No. 176

When the right one comes, the two halves will come together and be made whole! #WTROC

No. 177

When the right man comes, he will know how to close and seal the deal, with his lady! #WTROC

No. 178

When the right one comes, it won't make a difference who says I love you first it will happen with ease! #WTROC

No. 179

A man will do anything for a lady who speaks a sweet word to him and does not nag him! #WTROC

No. 180

Don't ignore the warning signs, when you see them! Say goodbye, before it goes any further! #WTROC

No. 181

Ladies, while you are waiting on him, don't sit idle while waiting. PREPARE! #WTROC

No. 182

Ladies don't spend your whole life waiting and become bitter and not better! #WTROC

No. 183

When the right man comes he will be your hero! #WTROC

No. 184

When the right one comes, they will be your biggest supporter and cheerleader! #WTROC

No. 185

When the right one comes, you won't just have companionship, but you will have friendship! #WTROC

No. 186

Ladies a man can't take you, where he's never been...maybe it's taking so long, because he's getting experience before he gets there! #WTROC

No. 187

If physical attraction is the only thing that attracted you then it will be the only thing that will keep you! It fades! #WTROC

No. 188

When the right man comes, he will add to what you already have going on! #WTROC

No. 189

When the right one comes, don't expect them to make you. They are there to complete you, not make you! #WTROC

No. 190

Finding you is the most important piece, to you finding the right one. #WTROC

No. 191

When the right man comes, he will value who you are and what you bring to the table! #WTROC

No. 192

High standards take longer to fulfill. Low standards can happen now! #WTROC

No. 193

Some people lowered their standards and got stuck with something they can't get out of! #WTROC

No. 194

Don't let people make you lower your standards for what you want out of a mate, because they don't have any standards #WTROC

No. 195

When the right man comes, you will be proud to call him yours! #WTROC

No. 196

When the right man comes, ladies, your days of regrets are over! #WTROC

No. 197

When the right one man comes you will take the risk that you wouldn't take before! #WTROC

No. 198

When the right man comes, they will unlock in you things that have been locked up for years! #WTROC

No. 199

When the right one comes, you will make it last forever and not a momentary feeling! #WTROC

No. 200

When the right comes, they will change your life forever! #WTROC

No. 201

When the right man comes, his lady will be the only one he desires #WTROC

No. 202

When the right one comes, you won't be pulling one way and they're pulling another! #WTROC

No. 203

When the right one comes along, you will know it, because you would have met all the "wrong" ones #WTROC

No. 204

When the right one comes, they would be able to pass all of your tests and requirements! #WTROC

No. 205

When the right one comes, your God will be their God and your people will be their people! Unity! #WTROC

No. 206

When the right one comes, you will work through the hard times and celebrate the good times! #WTROC

No. 207

When the right one comes, they won't disappoint you! #WTROC

No. 208

When the right one comes you will never think of another! #WTROC

No. 209

When the right one comes, they will love you in every way you will need to be, want to be and deserve to be loved! #WTROC

No. 210

When the right man comes, you no longer open yourself up to hurt, but you open up to be loved and appreciated! #WTROC

No. 211

When the right one comes, it won't matter who makes the most money. It will belong to you both! #WTROC

No. 212

When the right man comes, he will make you feel at peace and not on pins and needles! #WTROC

No. 213

Ladies, when the right man comes, he will not be intimidated by you, your status or what you already have! #WTROC

No. 214

When the right one comes they will never dishonor you but honor you at all times! #WTROC

No. 215

When the right one comes, you will be thankful for the gift that has been sent to you! #WTROC

No. 216

When the right one comes, communication will be a priority in the relationship. #WTROC

No. 217

When the right lady comes, she will not be with you, because of what you can do for her or give her. #WTROC

No. 218

When the right man comes, he will send chocolates, flowers and gifts, just because! #WTROC

No. 219

When the right man comes, you won't have to tell him how you want to be treated and taken care of. He will know. #WTROC

No. 220

When the right one comes, there's mutual respect and understanding for each other! #WTROC

No. 221

When the right one comes you both think about each other all the time! #WTROC

No. 222

When the right one comes it will be alright to be yourself at all times! #WTROC

No. 223

When the right lady comes, she will know the right words to say, at the right time to her man! #WTROC

No. 224

When the right man comes, he won't talk down to you, but build you up! #WTROC

No. 225

When the right one comes you will motivate and encourage each toward your goals! #WTROC

No. 226

You don't find the right one, you become the right one and the right one finds you! #WTROC

No. 227

When the right one comes, there is nothing that we cannot work out together! #WTROC

No. 228

When the right one comes, they will bring joy into your life and not sorrow! #WTROC

No. 229

When the right one comes, they will come with the qualities and integrity I have believed for them to have. #WTROC

No. 230

When the right man comes, he will come with vision for his life and ours as a unit! #WTROC

No. 231

We say the reason it's taking so long for the right one to come is that they're being prepared. Maybe the one being prepared is us! #WTROC

No. 232

Never want anyone who doesn't want you! Wrong one! #WTROC

No. 233

When the right one comes, it will be the right timing and the right one. #WTROC

No. 234

When the right one comes, you can't shake the feelings no matter how hard you try! #WTROC

No. 235

Would you rather be frustrated in waiting for them or be frustrated with the wrong one!?!?! #WTROC

No. 236

When right man comes, he will LOVE you just as you are, because real love won't require you to change who you are! #WTROC

No. 237

When the right man comes, you won't have to wait for him to get ready. He will come equipped and ready to be the man! #WTROC

No. 238

Don't let bad memories of the wrong one cause you to miss out on great new memories, with the right one! #WTROC

No. 239

When the right one comes, they may have looks, but they will also have wisdom! #WTROC

No. 240

When the right man comes, he will take his rightful place and lead as a king who he was created to be! #WTROC

No. 241

When the right one comes, it's always when you didn't expect them to! #WTROC

No. 242

When right man comes, he recognizes you're the right lady! #WTROC

No. 243

When the right man comes, you will allow him to be the MAN! #WTROC

No. 244

When the man comes, he is persistent and consistent with his pursuit! #WTROC

No. 245

When the right man comes, he will waste no time to tell you how he feels! #WTROC

No. 246

When the right man comes, he won't take no for answer! #WTROC

No. 247

When the right one comes, you will let your guard down and take the chance! #WTROC

No. 248

When the right one comes, they immediately peak your interest in a new and fresh way! #WTROC

No. 249

When the right one comes, there's something different you feel! #WTROC

No. 250

When the right one comes, you feel it even if you don't want them to know it at first! #WTROC

No. 251

For you to find the right one, it takes a little longer because there's only a few that #WTROC

No. 252

When the right one comes, they won't have two lives you will be there only life! #WTROC

No. 253

When the right one comes, you can't play the blame game. Blaming them for things for what others did to you! #WTROC

No. 254

If you don't know how to live and enjoy life, you won't know what to expect! Live it up now! #WTROC

No. 255

When the right one comes, you don't throw in their face what the wrong ones did to you! #WTROC

No. 256

When the right one comes, don't make them pay for all the wrong ones! #WTROC

No. 257

When the right one comes, you're not still trying to find yourself, after waiting to find them! #WTROC

No. 258

When the right man comes, he won't be an angel in public but a devil at home! #WTROC

No. 259

When the right one comes, they won't appear to be a blessing, but really a curse. They will be a blessing! #WTROC

No. 260

When the right one comes, they won't take backwards, but you will move forward together! #WTROC

No. 261

Don't settle for them just because everyone else has someone. You have no idea how miserable they might be! #WTROC

No. 262

When the right comes, you're not with them, because you feel like you're running out of time! #WTROC

No. 263

When the right one comes, it won't only be an emotional choice, but intelligent choice also! #WTROC

No. 264

When the right one comes, it won't be a forced fit. It will be an easy fit, for both! #WTROC

No. 265

When you find your SOUL mate.....They won't make you lose your MIND! #WTROC

No. 266

When the right one comes, they will know what to do when to do it and how to do it! #WTROC

No. 267

When the right one comes, you're looking at their maturity and not their looks. Looks can be deceiving. Good looks, empty head #WTROC

No. 268

When the right one comes, you're in it for the long haul not short term! #WTROC

No. 269

When the right one comes, you will be so grateful you waited on them! #WTROC

No. 270

When the right man comes, he won't put you on his arms just for a showpiece, because he knows she belongs by his side not behind. *#WTROC*

No. 271

Every woman wants to hear a man say, "Talk to me." Those are the sexiest 3 words you could ever say to a woman. Seriously, I hope you hear me. *#WTROC*

No. 272

When the right man comes, he won't mind admitting he's wrong and telling his lady he's sorry! *#WTROC*

No. 273

When the right woman comes, she's not in it for what she can get from him, but because she honestly is into him! *#WTROC*

No. 274

When the right man comes, you aren't worried about where he is at the moment, because you know where he's going in the future! *#WTROC*

No. 275

You know all the signs, but you want to ignore them because you want it to work! The right one is waiting for you. #WTROC

No. 276

Release the wrong one and you will attract the right one! #WTROC

No. 277

When the right man comes, you won't let miserable girlfriends talk you out of him! #WTROC

No. 278

When the right man comes, he will not be one dimensional! #WTROC

No. 279

Ladies... Never marry a man for what he HAS, instead marry him for who he IS in ALL seasons!!! #WTROC

No. 280

When the right one comes, you won't have think about if they're the right one or not! #WTROC

No. 281

You will never be with the right one, if you keep holding on to the wrong ones! #WTROC

No. 282

You can't find the right one, if you can't see them on the canvas of your imagination first! #WTROC

No. 283

If you want to keep playing around, the right one will never come. The right one is reserved for those who are ready! #WTROC

No. 284

When the right man comes, he will not see impossibilities, but say all things are possible for us! #WTROC

No. 285

When the right man comes, he will be a Dreamer! #WTROC

No. 286

When the right one comes, you won't be jealous of the other, because you are one and you can't be jealous of yourself! *#WTROC*

No. 287

When the right one comes, it will be mutual admiration for each other! *#WTROC*

No. 288

When the right one comes, you won't have to share them with another! *#WTROC*

No. 289

When the right man comes, he won't use his mouth to say I love you one day and cuss you out the next! *#WTROC*

No. 290

If you they keep you stressed out all the time, it's time to move on... not the one! *#WTROC*

No. 291

When the right one comes, you won't have mixed feelings about them you will know, this is it! #WTROC

No. 292

When the right one comes, it will be a matter of the heart and head! Not just emotions! #WTROC

No. 293

When the right man comes, you will feel different about him than anyone else you have met! #WTROC

No. 294

When the right one comes, they will be different from anyone you have dated before! #WTROC

No. 295

When the right man comes, he will have confidence in himself and you! #WTROC

No. 296

When the right one comes, you stop talking about old relationships and start talking about the new one, in your life. #WTROC

No. 297

When the right one comes, they won't allow you to lose yourself because of them! #WTROC

No. 298

When the right one comes, they will support you to the end! #WTROC

No. 299

When the right man comes in your life, he will stand up for you! #WTROC

No. 300

When the right one comes, you won't wait on someone to tell you, if they like you or not! #WTROC

No. 301

When right man comes, what's important to you will be important him! #WTROC

No. 302

You may say I don't have time for a relationship, but you will make time, when the right one comes! #WTROC

No. 303

When the right one comes, you will work hard to make it work! #WTROC

No. 304

When the right man comes, he won't just want to stimulate your mind, but your mind also! #WTROC

No. 305

When the right one comes you will rearrange your life and find time for them, because they are your new priority! #WTROC

No. 306

When the right one comes, you don't let family or friends get in between your relationship! #WTROC

No. 307

When right one comes, they won't want to waste a lot of time! #WTROC

No. 308

When the right one comes, they will be open and honest! #WTROC

No. 309

When the right one comes, they put closure to any past relationship you have still open! #WTROC

No. 310

When the right man comes, he will not just honor you with lip service, but with all of his substance he has! #WTROC

No. 311

When the right man comes, it won't be about I or me, but US! #WTROC

No. 312

When the right one comes, you will ask God why it took so long! #WTROC

No. 313

When the man comes, you will be the object of his affection! #WTROC

No. 314

When the right one comes, he or she will be what you dreamed of. Dreams do come true! #WTROC

No. 315

When the right man comes, he will make you feel safe and secure. You will know that he got u! #WTROC

No. 316

When right man comes, he will lighten your load not make it heavier! #WTROC

No. 317

When the right one comes, you will make decisions together! #WTROC

No. 318

When the right one comes, you will totally understand why the wrong ones weren't optional! #WTROC

No. 319

Don't mess up with the wrong one and lose the right one! #WTROC

No. 320

When the right one comes, both parties will be willing to invest time and treasure! #WTROC

No. 321

When the right one comes, it won't be constant friction, but it will flow in harmony! #WTROC

No. 322

When the right one comes, they will work with you and not against you! #WTROC

No. 323

This may sound hokey, but being in a relationship is not a destination, but a journey. I pray you are on the journey with the right one. #WTROC

No. 324

When the right one comes, they will have more positives about them than negative! #WTROC

No. 325

Who God has for you is for you...not just for a season, but for a lifetime, till death do us part! #WTROC

No. 326

When the right one comes, they won't just be a way to have sinless SEX, but you will really love them for them! #WTROC

No. 327

Men, when the right lady comes, it will be you and you only!! #WTROC

No. 328

When the right one comes, it will go way beyond sexual desire. It will be intellectual attraction! #WTROC

No. 329

When the right one comes, you won't just be infatuated with them, but you will like them! #WTROC

No. 330

Just because you are sexually attracted to someone, who makes your stomach flip and your heart beat fast, does not mean you are in love. #WTROC

No. 331

When the right one comes, you don't mind committing as long as there's equal commitment from each other! #WTROC

No. 332

What's the most important thing you need to discern #WTROC? DISCERNMENT!

No. 333

Be her TESTIMONY...Your COMMITMENT to honoring your name and hers shows your INTEGRITY, whether she is around you or when she ISN'T!!! #WTROC

No. 334

When the right man comes, a lady won't mind committing as long as she knows he's the one! #WTROC

No. 335

When the right one comes, you won't have to wonder whether they are feeling you or not!
#WTROC

No. 336

When the right man comes ladies, you lay down your insecurities and become secure! #WTROC

No. 337

When the right man comes, you won't mind being open and transparent about the way you feel about him! #WTROC

No. 338

When the right man comes, you won't mind losing control of feelings and emotions. You will let them flow! #WTROC

No. 339

When the right one comes, you will have many great days to share together. #WTROC

No. 340

When the right one comes, it won't be a hard push! It will flow! #WTROC

No. 341

When the right one comes, you won't have to convince them that they are the one, it will just flow! #WTROC

No. 342

Nothing wrong with exiting, but can somebody do it without being upset? Can you leave, because your season really is up and you're not mad? #WTROC

No. 343

When the right one comes, they will be sensitive to your total needs and wants! #WTROC

No. 344

When right lady comes, she will look, sound and act like what you have prayed and looked for! #WTROC

No. 345

When the right lady comes, she will do all she knows to do to please him! #WTROC

No. 346

When the right lady comes, she will not hide her feelings for her man! #WTROC

No. 347

When the right lady comes, she will appreciate what God has sent! #WTROC

No. 348

When the right man comes, he will take his rightful place and lead as a king who he was created to be! #WTROC

No. 349

When you start off with someone who is not equally yoked with you, you start an uphill journey.. Wait! #WTROC

No. 350

When the right man comes, he will lead in prayer praise and worship! You won't have to beg him! #WTROC

No. 351

When the right man comes, he will know God already and will not waver in his faith! #WTROC

No. 352

When the right man comes, he will lead in worshipping God! #WTROC

No. 353

When the right one comes, they won't be just a lot of talk they will back up what they say! #WTROC

No. 354

Don't just listen to what they say. Watch what they do! #WTROC

No. 355

When the right one comes, they will pay attention to details! #WTROC

No. 356

Man looking for the right one, ladies waiting and preparing for the right one! #*WTROC*

No. 357

Don't mistake the wrong one for the right one... big difference! #*WTROC*

No. 358

When the right man comes, he rises to the occasion and fills the void! #*WTROC*

No. 359

When the right man comes, he will know how to step up to the plate and do what he's supposed to do for you! #*WTROC*

No. 360

When the right man come ladies, you have to let him take his place as the man and enjoy all he brings to the table! #*WTROC*

No. 361

When the right man comes ladies, you have to adjust to now having a man to do all the things a man does for his lady! #WTROC

No. 362

When the right one comes, you gotta be open to new adventures! #WTROC

No. 363

When the right man comes, he will be a Man of Faith and Power! #WTROC

No. 364

When the right one comes, he will have manners and she will have class! #WTROC

No. 365

When the right one comes, your best days are ahead of you together! #WTROC

No. 366

When the right man comes, he will be a man of integrity! #WTROC

No. 367

When the right one comes, you need be right also! #WTROC

No. 368

When the right one comes, you never struggle with what to say! #WTROC

No. 369

Release yourself and your heart, to Love again! #WTROC

No. 370

When the right one comes, you work toward a common goal for the betterment of both of you! #WTROC

No. 371

When right one comes, you can work hard together, but also play hard together! #WTROC

No. 372

When the right one comes, you look forward to down time, so you can spend time with them! #WTROC

No. 373

When the right one comes, they will have your back no matter what! #WTROC

No. 374

When the right man comes, he will take you on a journey of a lifetime! #WTROC

No. 375

When the right one comes, a lady will let her guard down, but not until he proves worthy! #WTROC

No. 376

The right man will do whatever it takes, by any means necessary, to please her! #WTROC

No. 377

When the right one comes, you will feel the connection immediately! #wtroc

No. 378

When the right one comes, they will be able to see past your past! #WTROC

No. 379

When the right man comes, his aim is to protect your heart and never to break your heart! #WTROC

No. 380

When the right man comes, he will act like a real man! #WTROC

No. 381

When you meet someone, don't send your representative to date them... Be who you are, if they don't want you someone will! #WTROC

No. 382

When the right one comes, they won't play mind games with you! #WTROC

No. 383

If you have to change everything about u to be with someone, then they're not the one. #WTROC

No. 384

When the right one comes, they will love you right where you are! #WTROC

No. 385

When the right one comes, their motives will be pure with no hidden agendas! #WTROC

No. 386

When the right man comes, he won't be afraid of commitment! #WTROC

No. 387

When the right one comes, they will be honest and open with you! #WTROC

No. 388

When the right one comes, they will be thoughtful and considerate! #WTROC

No. 389

When the right one comes, they will make you first in their life, not second! #WTROC

No. 390

When the right one comes, they will be your partner working with you, not against you! #WTROC

No. 391

When you play games eventually, you will meet your match and they will beat you at what you thought you were a pro at! #WTROC

No. 392

When the right one comes, you don't let unhappy people get in between the relationship! #WTROC

No. 393

When the right one comes, you make them a priority in your life! #WTROC

No. 394

When the right man comes, he will do the chasing and you will be the lady you were born to be and able to enjoy it! #WTROC

No. 395

When the right one comes, both parties are willing to give a little to make things work! #WTROC

No. 396

When the right man comes, ladies, you won't have to do anything to get him he will be all in! #WTROC

No. 397

When the right one comes, you're determined to make it work! #WTROC

No. 398

When the right one comes, you will be open to change and new things! #WTROC

No. 399

When the right one comes, there's no obstacles to block it! #WTROC

No. 400

When the right one comes, you will be well prepared! #WTROC

No. 401

When the right one comes, you don't carry the last one in the relationship! #WTROC

No. 402

When the right man comes, his search is over he won't need another because you are the one! #WTROC

No. 403

When the right one comes, we don't argue and fuss we talk about it and continue the journey! #WTROC

No. 404

When the right one comes, we don't run. We work it out together and continue the journey! #WTROC

No. 405

When the right one comes, you don't have to rush the getting to know them! You want to enjoy every moment! #WTROC

No. 406

The "right one" will arrive at the right time on your life journey! #WTROC

No. 407

When the right one comes, you enjoy the journey of great possibilities you have together! #WTROC

No. 408

When the right one comes, you wake with a smile on your face, because you finally have the right one! #WTROC

No. 409

When the right one come, you go to bed thinking about then and you wake up thinking about them! #WTROC

No. 410

When the right man comes, he will make you take your game face off! #WTROC

No. 411

When the right man comes, he will make you say you're enjoying the connection! #WTROC

No. 412

When the right man comes, he will make a positive impression on you! #WTROC

No. 413

When the right man comes, he will make you feel like you have never felt in a relationship! #WTROC

No. 414

When the right one comes, you will be able to talk about anything with each other! #WTROC

No. 415

When right one comes, you will do all within your powers to hold on to what you've been waiting for! #WTROC

No. 416

When the right one comes, you will do all within your power to keep outsiders just that outside! #WTROC

No. 417

When the right man comes, you will be able to take the guard off your heart and love again! #WTROC

No. 418

When the right one comes, you won't have to worry about your heart being broken again. You will feel safe! #WTROC

No. 419

When the right one comes, there will be consistency in the relationship! #WTROC

No. 420

When the right one comes, they won't be self-centered, but their desire will be to please you! #WTROC

No. 421

When the right one comes, they will sit you down and you will say the wait is over! #WTROC

No. 422

When the right one comes, they should be confirmation to what you have been believing and waiting to come! #WTROC

No. 423

When the right one comes, they should be an upgrade ... Not a downgrade! #WTROC

No. 424

Lord, give us quick discernment to know the wrong one! #WTROC

No. 425

When the right one comes, God would have gotten them ready for you! They will be answered prayer! #WTROC

No. 426

Just when you think you know someone, then you realized you REALLY don't!! #WTROC

No. 427

When the right one comes, you won't have to deal with the foolishness you dealt with in the past. #WTROC

No. 428

When the right one comes, it won't be a one sided relationship. There will be equality! #WTROC

No. 429

When the right lady, comes she will love her man unconditionally! #WTROC

No. 430

When the right man comes, he won't disrespect his lady! #WTROC

No. 431

When the right man comes, you will be the one and only lady, in his life! #WTROC

No. 432

When the right man finds the right lady, it won't take years to close the deal! #WTROC

No. 433

When the right Man comes, he will put a ring on it! #WTROC

No. 434

When the right one comes, you will both realize there will be good days and bad days, but they will be fine as long as you got each other's back. #WTROC

No. 435

When the right one comes, you can be as transparent as you want to be and not worrying if they will judge you! #WTROC

No. 436

When the man comes, he will ask for a list of your favorite things and work on it item by item! #WTROC

No. 437

When the right man comes, he will send flowers just because.... #WTROC

No. 438

When the right one comes, they will be your greatest encourager! #WTROC

No. 439

When the right man comes, you will appreciate him and all he does for you! #WTROC

No. 440

When the right one comes, it will be about you and them and you won't let outside forces get in between the bond you have! #WTROC

No. 441

When the right man comes, you won't run him away like the wrong ones! #WTROC

No. 442

When the right one comes, they will take however long it takes to get know you and be friends! #WTROC

No. 443

When the right man comes, he will know how to talk to you! #WTROC

No. 444

When the right one comes, they would have already unpacked all their past baggage! #WTROC

No. 445

Is it possible you could be with the wrong one and the right one could be right under your nose?? I'm just saying? #WTROC

No. 446

Is it possible who you think may be the wrong one could be the right one? I'm just saying. #WTROC

No. 447

You will only know the right one, because you had so many wrong ones! #WTROC

No. 448

When the right one comes, you can build a future together that will last a life time! #WTROC

No. 449

When the right man comes, he will make you feel safe and secure! #WTROC

No. 450

When the right man comes, ladies all fears of being hurt again will leave! #WTROC

No. 451

When the right one comes, they will make the Long journey worth it! #WTROC

No. 452

When the right man comes, you will be the envy of all the girls! #WTROC

No. 453

When the right one comes, you will want to spend a lifetime with them! #WTROC

No. 454

You can't ask for something and not be ready to receive! Are you truly ready for the right one to come? #WTROC

No. 455

When the right one comes, you would have made space for them in your entire life! #WTROC

No. 456

When the right one comes, you gotta be ready for them! #WTROC

No. 457

When the right one comes, they will take your breath away! #WTROC

No. 458

When the right one comes, you will complete one another! #WTROC

No. 459

When the right one comes, they will know what to say, how to say it and when to say it! #WTROC

No. 460

When the right one comes, you will wish for them to always be around and not to stay away! #WTROC

No. 461

When the right one comes, your life turns for the better not into a nightmare! #WTROC

No. 462

When the right one comes, you will never second guess, if they are the right one. It will speak for itself! #WTROC

No. 463

When right man comes, he's a man and not a boy! #WTROC

No. 464

When the right man comes, he's gotten all the play and game out! #WTROC

No. 465

When the right man comes, he will be sure that you are the one! #WTROC

No. 466

When the right one comes, you can weather the storm together! #WTROC

No. 467

Ladies, stop waiting on a man to validate the woman you already are! #WTROC

No. 468

When the right man comes, his lady will have respect for him, because he has mutual respect for her! #WTROC

No. 469

When the right one comes, you will agree to disagree! #WTROC

No. 470

When the right one comes, you will both work together for the success of each other's dreams! #WTROC

No. 471

When the right one comes, they won't be judgmental of you, but living with grace! #WTROC

No. 472

When the right one comes, there will be nothing that's withheld from one another! #WTROC

No. 473

When the right one comes, they will know how to apologize and they will also know how to forgive. #WTROC

No. 474

When the right one comes, you will make necessary adjustments to make it work without changing your entire life! #WTROC

No. 475

When the right one comes, they will believe in us! #WTROC

No. 476

When the right man comes, he will celebrate the Woman that you are! *#WTROC*

No. 477

When the right man comes, he knows the difference between Sex and Romance! *#WTROC*

No. 478

When the right man comes, he will want more than just your body. He will want everything about u *#WTROC*

No. 479

When the right one comes, you won't let anyone come between you and them! *#WTROC*

No. 480

When the right one comes, you will be thankful that you didn't settle. *#WTROC*

No. 481

When the right man comes, he will make you feel so secure that even, when he's not around it will feel like it! #WTROC

No. 482

I want to encourage you to know that there is a "right one" tailored made, just for you. Are you ready to receive them? #WTROC

No. 483

When the right man comes, his lady will appreciate him because of all she had go to through to get to him! #WTROC

No. 484

When the right one comes, they will take you where you never been to get what you never had to do what you've never done! #WTROC

No. 485

When the right man comes, he will have patience to listen to his lady! #WTROC

No. 486

When the right man comes, his number one aim will be to please his lady, in every way every day! #WTROC

No. 487

Finding the right one is an exploration through all the wrong ones! But #WTROC you will know it!

No. 488

When the one comes, they will want you to be the best version of you possible! #WTROC

No. 489

When the right lady comes, she won't come as angry and bitter woman #WTROC

No. 490

When the right one comes, every memory will be lasting until the next time you're together! #WTROC

No. 491

When the right man comes, you will know it because he will sound like what you been waiting on! #WTROC

No. 492

When the right one comes, they will equally put their all into the relationship! #WTROC

No. 493

When the right lady comes, she will believe in her man! #WTROC

No. 494

When the right lady comes, she will know how to cook! #WTROC

No. 495

When the right lady comes, she won't be afraid of the word submission, because she understands it doesn't mean control! #WTROC

No. 496

When the right lady comes, she won't come with a lot of baggage that hasn't been unpacked! #WTROC

No. 497

When the right lady comes, she will honor you as the head! #WTROC

No. 498

When the right one comes, they let you be who you were born to be and not what they want u to be! #WTROC

No. 499

When the right one comes, you will be up late talking to them falling asleep! #WTROC

No. 500

If the right one had come, you probably would be up falling asleep on the phone with them right now! Lol #WTROC

No. 501

When the right man comes, no one else matters! #WTROC

No. 502

When the right man comes, nothing else will matter! #WTROC

No. 503

When the right man comes, you will be the only option he has! #WTROC

No. 504

When the right one comes, they won't expect for you to be perfect. They accept you just for who you are! #WTROC

No. 505

When the right one comes, they don't mind taking responsibility for their actions! #WTROC

No. 506

When the right man comes, he will share everything he has and won't withhold anything to please his lady! #WTROC

No. 507

When you get tired of the wrong ones, you will wait for the #WTROC

No. 508

When the right one comes, it won't be about any one any more, but you! #WTROC

No. 509

When the right man comes, he will have vision for himself and for his family's life! #WTROC

No. 510

When the right man comes, he will be a spiritual man! #WTROC

No. 511

When the right man comes, he will be a praying man and lead his family into prayer! #WTROC

No. 512

When the right man comes, he will love God first with all his heart and won't have any problem loving you! #WTROC

No. 513

When the right one comes, you will worship together and there won't any division! #WTROC

No. 514

When a lady finds the right man, she will do all she can to support him! #WTROC

No. 515

When the right man comes, he won't just act like he's listening, but he will interested in what you are saying! #WTROC

No. 516

When the right one comes, they will fill a void in your life! #WTROC

No. 517

When the right man comes, he won't take all day to put a rock on your finger! #WTROC

No. 518

When the right man comes, ladies, you won't have to tell him what you need or want. He will be so in tune that you will have it, before you can say it! #WTROC

No. 519

When the right one comes, he won't still be a mama's boy, but your MAN! *#WTROC*

No. 520

When the right man comes, he won't need you to affirm who he is. He will already know! *#WTROC*

No. 521

When the right man comes and finds you, he won't be still trying to find himself! *#WTROC*

No. 522

When the right one comes after pleasing God, they will do all they can to please you! *#WTROC*

No. 523

When the right one comes, they won't make excuses about spending the weekend together! *#WTROC*

No. 524

When you find the right one, they will go the extra mile for you!! *#WTROC*

No. 525

When the right man comes, ladies, he will tell everybody about you and take you everywhere, because he found the right one! #WTROC

No. 526

When a man finds the right lady, he will shower her with affection and love privately and publicly! #WTROC

No. 527

When a lady finds the right man, she won't continue to play hard to get! #WTROC

No. 528

When a man finds the right lady, he will love her with every fiber of his being! #WTROC

No. 529

When the right one comes, you will love each other unconditionally! #WTROC

No. 530

When the right one comes, the communications is open and honest #WTROC

No. 531

When the right one comes, you feel each other's up's and down's, without having to say anything! #WTROC

No. 532

When the right one comes, they won't be selfish! #WTROC

No. 533

When right one comes, they will tell you the truth no matter what! #WTROC

No. 534

When the right one comes, their word will be their bond! #WTROC

No. 535

When the right one comes, they won't lie to you! #WTROC

No. 536

When the right one comes, you will not have to force your way into their life! #WTROC

No. 537

When the right one comes, they will make you feel secure, in every area of your life! #WTROC

No. 538

Maybe that's why we're single, because there's a lot that goes into #WTROC! Haha! For real!

No. 539

It's not all about you and how busy you are! If you genuinely care about someone, you will make an effort to be in their life!! #WTROC

No. 540

When the right one comes, it will be a pleasure spending time with them, rather than a duty! #WTROC

No. 541

When the right one comes, there will more good days than bad together! #WTROC

No. 542

When the right one comes, you will have great memories to share of many yesterday's! #WTROC

No. 543

When the right one comes, you will make great memories together! #WTROC

No. 544

When the right one comes, you will be a part of each other's world! #WTROC

No. 545

When the right comes, both parties will know! It will not be one sided! #WTROC

No. 546

Focus in what you want. It will help to know what you don't want! #WTROC

No. 547

When the right man comes, ladies you won't have to wonder how he feels about you. He will tell you every chance he gets! #WTROC

No. 548

When the right man comes, ladies, he will captivate every part of your being! #WTROC

No. 549

When the right one comes, you won't have to go out alone again! #WTROC

No. 550

When the right one comes, you don't have to be who they want you to be, because you are what they want just as you are! #WTROC

No. 551

When the right one comes, you will be allowed to finally be you! #WTROC

No. 552

When the right one comes, they will support your every dream! #WTROC

No. 553

When the right one comes they won't frustrate you! #WTROC

No. 554

When the right man comes, he won't allow insecurities to stay around the lady he's with! #WTROC

No. 555

When the right one comes, you won't have to talk them every minute, but will make every minute count when you do speak to each other! #WTROC

No. 556

When the right one comes, you will want to spend every free moment you have with them! #WTROC

No. 557

When right man comes, ladies, he will wake up things that's been dormant in you for years! #WTROC

No. 558

When the right man comes, ladies, he will rock your world! #WTROC

No. 559

When the right one comes, haters will be hating on you, because you have the right one! #WTROC

No. 560

When the right man comes, if he leads right she will follow right! #WTROC

No. 561

When right one comes, you will want to make up for all the lost time you invested, in losers! #WTROC

No. 562

When the right man comes, he will make you think you are the only one in the world! #WTROC

No. 563

When the right one comes, you will have no problem telling the others to go! #WTROC

No. 564

When the right man comes, he won't physically or verbally abuse you! #WTROC

No. 565

When the right man comes, he will build his lady up and never tears her down! #WTROC

No. 566

When right one comes, there is harmony! #WTROC

No. 567

When the right one comes, you don't have an issue being accountable to one another! #WTROC

No. 568

When the right one comes, you work together on each other's goals! #WTROC

No. 569

When the right one comes, they will be a help to you and not a hindrance! #WTROC

No. 570

When the right one comes, they will like you just the way you are! #WTROC

No. 571

When the right one comes, they will erase all the wrong ones from your mind! #WTROC

No. 572

When the right one comes, they will enhance your happiness! #WTROC

No. 573

When the right one comes, you will do things you said you would never do, because they're the right one! #WTROC

No. 574

When the right one comes, you won't second guess it. All doubts will be settled! #WTROC

No. 575

When a man finds the right lady, he won't let her go out looking less than him! #WTROC

No. 576

When man finds the right lady, he only has eyes for her! #WTROC

No. 577

When the right one comes, you don't have to smother them, because you know your relationship is secure! #WTROC

No. 578

When the right one comes, the first person you think about after thanking God for the day is them! #WTROC

No. 579

When the right one comes, you wake up in the morning with a smile on your face because you just thought about them! #WTROC

No. 580

When a man finds the right lady, he will love her every way she wants to be loved! #WTROC

No. 581

When the right one comes, they will know how to love you! #WTROC

No. 582

When a man finds the right lady, he will be her Priest, Provider and Protector! #WTROC

No. 583

When the right one comes, everything is shared and nothing is held back! #WTROC

No. 584

When the right one comes, there will a bond that no one can break, not even family or friends! #WTROC

No. 585

When the right one comes, there is nothing you won't share with one another! #WTROC

No. 586

When the right one comes, their pain will be your pain! #WTROC

No. 587

When the right one comes, you will be able to talk about anything with them! #WTROC

No. 588

When the right one comes, honesty and trust won't be an issue! #WTROC

No. 589

When the right one comes, you overcome the fear of them being the wrong one! #WTROC

No. 590

When the right one comes, it won't be a forced situation. Both parties will feel it! #WTROC

No. 591

When a man finds the right lady, she will bring out the best in him! #WTROC

No. 592

When a man finds the right lady, she will encourage support and build him up to make him feel like he can do anything! #WTROC

No. 593

When a man finds the right lady, she will know the mood he's in the moment he walks in the door! #WTROC

No. 594

When a man finds the right lady, she will speak to every fiber of his being! #WTROC

No. 595

When the right one comes, you will be best friends first. #WTROC

No. 596

When the right one comes, there will be no DRAMA! #WTROC

No. 597

When the right one comes, they won't make chase after them! #WTROC

No. 598

When the right one comes, they will allow you to be the creative you that you were born to be! #WTROC

No. 599

So many stay single, because they have no time to teach someone who's supposed to be grown! #WTROC

No. 600

When the right one comes, they will compliment what you are already doing! #WTROC

No. 601

When the right one comes, you won't have to school them. They have already graduated! #WTROC

121

No. 602

When the right one comes, they won't have to make many concessions, if any! #WTROC

No. 603

When the right one comes, they like you for who you are and not what you do! #WTROC

No. 604

When the right one comes, they will become your No.1 Cheerleader! #WTROC

No. 605

Be careful who you share your dreams with, everybody is not your Cheerleader! #WTROC

No. 606

When the right one comes, there will be a chemistry like you have not felt with any other! #WTROC

No. 607

When the right one comes, there is mutual admiration and respect! #WTROC

No. 608

When the right one comes, you're not ashamed to tell and show everybody you finally got the right one! #WTROC

No. 609

When the right one comes, you don't have to tell them how to treat you! They already know! #WTROC

No. 610

Everyone wants The Right One, but if we continue to be afraid we may miss them, because we won't take that chance! #WTROC

No. 611

When the right man comes, he will be honest about where he's at in his life and you will accept where he's at, because you see possibility! #WTROC

No. 612

When the right on comes, they complement what you are doing already! #WTROC

No. 613

When the right one comes, you will look at them and say WOW it was worth the wait! #WTROC

No. 614

When a man finds the right lady, she will open things up in him that he didn't even know was in him. Only when he finds the right one! #WTROC

No. 615

When a man finds the right one, she completes him! #WTROC

No. 616

When a man finds the right lady, things he's been trying to do become easier! #WTROC

No. 617

When a man finds the right one, his life becomes complete! #WTROC

No. 618

When the right one comes, you will love them from the inside out! #WTROC

No. 619

When the right one comes, the outer might draw us, but the inner will keep you! #WTROC

No. 620

When the right one comes, you're not afraid to Love! #WTROC

No. 621

When the right one comes, it won't be a fix me up project! #WTROC

No. 622

When the right man comes, you won't have to fix him up. He will already come as you need and want him! #WTROC

No. 623

Ladies, you are good enough. Pretty enough. He's trying to step up his game to be good enough for you. Wait on him - the right one is coming #WTROC

No. 624

Ladies, the only thing a guy should want to change about you is your Last Name... All other candidates can keep it moving. Lol #love #WTROC

No. 625

When the right man comes, he will reaffirm who you know you are already! #WTROC

No. 626

When the right man comes, he will build up his lady and not tear her down! #WTROC

No. 627

Ladies, if you build him up with your words and actions, he will desire you in his life. #WTROC

No. 628

When the right one comes, you will appreciate them, because of how long it God to prepare both of you! #WTROC

No. 629

When the right man comes and you go to dinner all you have to do is stand by your seat and he will do the rest! #WTROC

No. 630

When the right man comes, you no longer open doors! #WTROC

No. 631

When the right one comes all the dots are connected why the others were the wrong ones! #WTROC

No. 632

When the right one comes, you finally won't ask anyone their opinion about them, because they are the right one! #WTROC

No. 633

When a man finds the right one, he will open up because he has found his friend for life! #WTROC

No. 634

When the right one comes, feelings will be mutual and not one sided! #WTROC

No. 635

When the right one comes, you will push each other to greatness! #WTROC

No. 636

When the right one comes, you will both be interested, in each other's destiny! #WTROC

No. 637

When you find the right one, you don't have to keep running after them! #WTROC

No. 638

When the right one comes, they will be everything you prayed for and believed in faith for, because anything else is not the right one! #WTROC

No. 639

When the right one comes, they will celebrate who you are and not just tolerate you! #WTROC

No. 640

When the right man comes, he won't be jealous of her success! He will know it only complements his success! #WTROC

No. 641

I hope for the last two days someone has been inspired from hearing me think out loud about #WTROC

No. 642

When the right one comes, they will have enough influence to make you change. What's not right! #WTROC

No. 643

When the right one comes, they will hold your attention! #WTROC

No. 644

When man finds the right one, there is no one more beautiful than her! #WTROC

No. 645

When the right one comes, they capture your attention and affection! #WTROC

No. 646

When you find the right one, all GAMES cease! #WTROC

No. 647

When a man finds the right one, he will introduce as his! #WTROC

No. 648

When a man finds the right one, you won't have to ask him the status of the relationship he will make it known! #WTROC

No. 649

When the right one comes, they won't have to ask when will I see you again? #WTROC

No. 650

When the right one comes, when they talk it will be soothing and not nagging #WTROC

No. 651

When the right one comes, it's not forced it just fits!
#WTROC

No. 652

When the right one comes, you either change your
number and you erase all numbers without them
asking you too! #WTROC

No. 653

When the right one comes, they won't have to say
I'm the one! #WTROC

No. 654

When you find the right one, they're not in
competition with you! #WTROC

No. 655

When you find the right one, you wake up with them
on your mind with a smile! #WTROC

No. 656

When man finds the right one, he finds a good thing
and obtains favor from the Lord! #WTROC

No. 657

When a man finds the right one, he will do all he can to make her happy! #WTROC

No. 658

When a woman finds the right one, she will call him lord as Sarah called Abram! #WTROC

No. 659

When a woman finds the right one, there is nothing she won't do to make him feel like the ONE! #WTROC

No. 660

When a man finds the right one, he makes sure they live a balanced life! #WTROC

No. 661

When a man finds the right one, he will make it last forever! #WTROC

No. 662

When a man finds the right one, she won't have to worry about another woman, because she's the only one! #WTROC

No. 663

The RIGHT woman will make a man at BETTER everything! #WTROC

No. 664

When a man finds the right one, he won't be able to keep his eyes off of her! #WTROC

No. 665

When a man finds the right one, she won't have to ask him for anything and he will give her everything! #WTROC

No. 666

When a man finds the right one, he will tell everyone including his buddies! #WTROC

No. 667

Someday, I will meet a man who loves me for who I am and supports all my dreams. And I'll think, "Something must be wrong with this one." #WTROC

No. 668

When you find the right one, not only you will know it but people will look at you and say what a couple! #WTROC

No. 670

When a man finds the one, flowers are sent just because! #WTROC

No. 671

When a man finds the right one, it doesn't matter whether or not she has makeup on or not! #WTROC

No. 672

When you find the right one, the room can be full but you spot them thru the crowd! #WTROC

No. 673

When you find the right one, they don't have to ask you when we are seeing each other again! #WTROC

No. 674

When you find the right one, you think of them on two occasions and that's day and night! #WTROC

No. 675

If you are like me, you know what the right one feels like ... Just haven't found it! #WTROC

No. 676

When you find the right one, it doesn't take all day to know it! #WTROC

No. 677

When a man finds the right one, she won't have to ask him say I Love you! #WTROC

No. 678

When a man finds the right one, he will make time for her! No matter how busy he is! #WTROC

No. 679

When you find the right one, you may argue in the am, but you make up by pm! #WTROC

No. 680

When a man finds the right one, she won't have to ask what her status is, in his life. He will show her! #WTROC

No. 681

When a man knows it's the right one, she becomes queen of his throne! #WTROC

No. 682

When it's the right one, its equal admiration and not one sided! #WTROC

No. 683

When the right one comes, you smile, when you think about them! #WTROC

No. 684

When the right one comes, you want to spend every free moment you have! #WTROC

No. 685

When the right one comes, they're your best friend and confidant! #WTROC

No. 686

When the right one comes, you still smell their scent in the evening, when you were around them in the morning! #WTROC

No. 687

When the right one comes, your eyes cease to roam! #WTROC

No. 688

When the right one comes, the search is over! #WTROC

No. 689

When the right one comes, they won't have to ask for what they want or need! #WTROC

No. 690

When the right one comes, you won't look for another! #WTROC

No. 691

When the right one comes, they will take you back to your teenage days, when you fell asleep on the phone with them. #WTROC

No. 692

When the right one comes, you won't want to look at another! #WTROC

Now, journal your very own
"When The Right One Comes" quotes.
What do you expect in your "right one?"
#WTROC

1._____
_____
_____
_____
_____

2._____
_____
_____
_____
_____

3._____
_____
_____
_____
_____

4._____
_____
_____
_____
_____

5._____
_____
_____
_____
_____

6._____
_____
_____
_____
_____

7._____
_____
_____
_____
_____

8._____
_____
_____
_____
_____

9._____
_____
_____
_____
_____

10._____
_____
_____
_____
_____

11._____
_____
_____
_____
_____

12._____

_____
_____
_____
_____

13._____

_____
_____
_____
_____

14._____

_____
_____
_____
_____

15._____

_____
_____
_____
_____

16._____
_____
_____
_____
_____

17._____
_____
_____
_____
_____

18._____
_____
_____
_____
_____

19._____
_____
_____
_____
_____

20._____

_____

_____

_____

_____

21._____

_____

_____

_____

_____

22._____

_____

_____

_____

_____

23._____

_____

_____

_____

_____

24._____
_____
_____
_____
_____
_____

25._____
_____
_____
_____
_____
_____

Contact Information

To contact or book Bishop Greg M. Davis for your next event, go to:

PO Box 44072 Detroit, MI 48244
www.gregdavisshow.com
Download The Greg Davis App available in Android and Apple Store
For Booking: gregdavisshow@gmail.com

Listen to the greg davis radio show on:
Gospel 860
WEHA 88.7
WCCD Am 1000
The Tune In App
Radio 1000 App
www.mixcloud.com/gregdavisshow

Watch the greg davis show on:
www.watchimpact.com
Comcast 400
Dish 256

Follow Bishop Greg Davis:
Twitter: @bishopgregdavis
Instagram: @bishopgregdavis
Facebook: www.facebook.com/Bishop-Greg-Davis
www.youtube.com/gregdavisshow

Made in the USA
Las Vegas, NV
06 June 2021